Written by
Susan Kilpatrick

Editor: Carla Hamaguchi
Illustrator: Catherine Yuh Rader
Cover Photographer: Michael Jarrett
Cover Illustrator: Kimberlee Graves
Designer: Moonhee Pak
Cover Designer: Moonhee Pak
Art Director: Tom Cochrane
Project Director: Carolea Williams

Thanks to my teaching colleagues and good friends, Pat Highfill, Mary Kate Hagmann, and Sheri Ryan, for sharing their ideas with me.

100TH DAY WORRIES by Margery Cuyler, illustrated by Arthur Howard.
Text copyright © 2000 by Margery Cuyler. Illustrations copyright © 2000 by Arthur Howard.
Used with permission of Simon & Schuster Books for Young Readers, an imprint of Simon & Schuster Children's Publishing.

Table of Contents

Writing Lessons Using Literature Models

USE SPECIFIC DETAILS TO FOCUS ON A TOPIC

USE ADJECTIVES AND/OR DESCRIPTIVE DETAILS

ARRANGE IDEAS CHRONOLOGICALLY OR IN A LOGICAL ORDER

USE DIALOGUE TO SHOW CHARACTERS' THOUGHTS AND FEELINGS

Introduction

Developing Young Authors K–1 provides over 20 step-by-step lessons that feature a favorite literature selection to model good writing. Each lesson is designed to encourage students to create text innovations. Text innovations are sentences or stories based on the structure of existing text. This type of writing experience will help students gain confidence in their writing, build their vocabulary, develop critical writing skills, and begin to see themselves as young authors. Once this happens, students are ready to tackle more advanced writing assignments such as short narrative writing, responses to literature, and even Writer's Workshop.

Each lesson is based on a familiar children's book. These books were selected because they inspire students in their own writing and serve as models of specific characteristics of good writing, form, and style. The literature selections in *Developing Young Authors K–1* are grouped in four categories based on which writing skill is most prominently modeled in each book. (Additional writing traits are noted on the first page of each lesson, where appropriate.)

Read the literature selections to the class, and use the discussion and prewriting activities to teach students to recognize familiar writing and the characteristics of good books and to encourage them to make connections between the story and their own experiences. Follow the detailed guidelines to model each text innovation and create a supportive environment where students of all abilities can confidently complete the writing activity. Each lesson includes a reproducible student page and a reproducible book cover. Compile the completed student pages and cover into class or individual books—valuable classroom resources that the student authors will eagerly read again and again.

The lessons in *Developing Young Authors K–1* enable students to use their prior knowledge and personal experiences to make significant connections with the literature selections. As students begin to make this reading–writing connection, they gradually gain the skills and confidence to write their own stories. Soon students will be on their way toward becoming more proficient writers.

Benefits of Text Innovation Lessons

Text innovations are sentences or stories based on the structure of existing text. Students create a text innovation by writing their own words or phrases in a sentence frame. The lessons in *Developing Young Authors K–1* invite students to create text innovations based on the patterns found in familiar children's books. These lessons include the following benefits:

- Students enhance their reading skills by listening to and/or reading the literature.

- Students generate personal writing topics.

- Students begin to make the reading–writing connection.

- Students work with models of good sentence structure.

- Students draw on prior knowledge and experience when they write.

- The student-written books become a valuable classroom resource as they are read and reread by the student authors.

- Students begin to see themselves as authors and gradually gain confidence to write their own stories.

- Students enhance their reading comprehension by reading the text and discussing its meaning.

- Students have many opportunities to build vocabulary as they brainstorm ideas and discuss individual responses.

- Students work toward becoming more proficient at the conventions of writing.

- Students develop listening skills as they listen for the story pattern or the way the author begins and ends sentences.

- Students begin to extend their ideas and add more detail to their writing.

- English language learners and struggling readers and writers receive guided instruction during the reading of the book and the follow-up activity.

Connections to Reading/Language Arts Standards

Use the activities in *Developing Young Authors K–1* to help students reach some of your state's required educational expectations. Standards vary by state; the following is a compilation of skills required by many states at the kindergarten and first-grade levels. Check your state standards for more specific information.

READING

- Students know about letters, words, and sounds. They apply this knowledge to read simple sentences.

- Students have an understanding of concepts about print, phonemic awareness, decoding, and word recognition.

- Students describe common objects and events in general and specific language.

- Students connect the information and events in texts to life experiences.

- Students understand the basic features of reading. They select letter patterns and know how to translate them into spoken language by using phonics, syllabication, and word parts. They apply this knowledge to achieve fluent oral and silent reading.

- Students read aloud with fluency in a manner that sounds like natural speech.

WRITING

- Students use letters and phonetically spelled words to write about experiences, stories, people, objects, or events.

- Students apply writing conventions appropriate to their grade level (e.g., upper/lowercase letters, spaces, conventional spelling, punctuation, and capitalization).

- Students write words and brief sentences that are legible.

- Students write and speak in complete, coherent sentences.

- Students use descriptive words when writing.

- Students organize their ideas chronologically.

- Students use basic text structure that gives the reader a clear sense of purpose.

Developing Literacy Awareness

The activities presented in *Developing Young Authors K–1* will help students develop literacy awareness. The suggested literature selections provide easy reading and models for student writing. Once students recognize the author's pattern, they can use the pattern to create their own version of the text.

TYPES OF BOOKS

Predictable patterned stories are built on accumulated repetitions that students will soon be able to chant while you read. Some books have repetitive refrains (e.g., *King Bidgood's in the Bathtub*).

Books with rhymed text provide students with the opportunity to focus on hearing the sounds of rhyming words in context. Studies show improvement in students' awareness of sounds leads to greater success in reading.

Rebus stories have pictures substituted for some words. These types of books (e.g., *The Jacket I Wear in the Snow*) are good resources for creating successful reading experiences. The pictures provide clues and convey the meaning that gives support to the emergent reader.

CONCEPTS ABOUT PRINT

Concepts about print refers to the understanding of what print represents and how it works. Text innovations are an excellent way to teach students the skills related to concepts about print. Students put in to practice such skills as directionality, one-to-one correspondence, spacing, using punctuation marks, and making the illustrations match the text.

VOCABULARY DEVELOPMENT

Listening to and reading good literature helps students expand their vocabulary. During the lessons, point out the use of imaginative language; the vivid, expressive words; and/or the less familiar words. Discuss and define words as needed. However, do not spend a lot of time defining words while reading the text. Allow students to hear the fluent reading of the story so they can focus on the pattern, main ideas, and/or author's style.

Lessons at a Glance

Each literature selection in *Developing Young Authors K–1* includes a step-by-step lesson that features a whole-class reading and discussion, a prewriting activity, the writing of a student text innovation, and the creation of a class or an individual book. Use the literature selections to introduce, model, and have students practice a writing skill, or use the chart on page 9 to choose a lesson that coordinates with a particular theme or unit of study. The first page of each lesson includes the following information to help you prepare and implement the activities for that book's text innovation.

LITERATURE SELECTION

Each lesson is based on a familiar children's book. Each book is ideal for reading aloud to the class. Read the brief synopsis to familiarize yourself with the story.

KEY WRITING SKILL

All fictional literature books possess—to some degree—the basic elements of plot, character, setting, and style. Each literature selection exemplifies and serves as a model of one or more specific writing skills for students to study and then practice in their own writing. This section lists one or more writing skills for you to point out and discuss with students after you read the book to the class. Students will become more proficient writers as they learn to recognize the characteristics of good books and begin to apply this knowledge to their own writing.

PREWRITING

Each lesson describes a prewriting activity designed to have students brainstorm a list of ideas that they can use to create their text innovation. Record their responses on the chalkboard, or write them on chart paper and post it. The brainstorm list will enhance your print-rich environment as well as validate students' responses, which in turn encourages them to participate in future brainstorm sessions. Add illustrations to the list for less proficient readers and writers. This will serve as a visual clue for students who independently reread the list.

The prewriting activity will encourage students to think about the content of the story they just heard and help them connect it to their own lives through class discussion and brainstorming. This is also a good time to discuss characteristics of the story (e.g., setting, plot), to check for students' reading comprehension by asking them specific questions about the story, and to discuss and define any words students struggled with or did not know.

WRITING

Each lesson includes one or more reproducible student pages. Read the reproducible pages to the class so students are familiar with the text. Model on the chalkboard or chart paper how to write and complete the frame(s) for each text innovation. Reread the completed sentences with the class. Have students use the brainstorm list or chart to help them complete their own text innovations. Then, invite them to illustrate their writing.

Invite younger students to dictate their sentence. Dictation shows students what it means to be a writer. The student is free to focus on the sentence he or she is completing. The objective of dictation is to allow students to focus on creativity, use their imagination, and create stories. This is a vital process for all writers. Write the student's words with a yellow marker. Then, have the student say the name of each letter as he or she traces over it. This process will help students with letter recognition and letter writing.

MAKING A BOOK

Collect all the completed pages, and combine them in a class book. Make a copy of the reproducible cover. Have a student volunteer color it. Glue the cover to a piece of construction paper, and laminate it. Punch holes through one side of the pages, and bind them with brads, ribbon, or yarn.

Place the completed class books in the classroom library, and invite students to independently read them. Create a special place for these books by decorating a large box or bin. Label the box *Our Class Books*. Students will love reading and rereading these books. They will feel like successful readers because they will be able to read the books on their own.

Theme	King Bidgood's in the Bathtub	Green Eggs and Ham	When I Was Five	The Very Hungry Caterpillar	Ten Black Dots	The Jacket I Wear in the Snow	The Itsy Bitsy Spider	If You Give a Mouse a Cookie	A House Is a House for Me	Mary Wore Her Red Dress and Henry Wore His Green Sneakers	Lunch	It Looked Like Spilt Milk	I Went Walking	Goodnight Moon	Caps, Hats, Socks, and Mittens	Brown Bear, Brown Bear, What Do You See?	When I Get Bigger	When Cows Come Home	Some Things Go Together	Eating the Alphabet: Fruits & Vegetables from A to Z	The Bag I'm Taking to Grandma's	100th Day Worries...
100th day of school																						●
alphabet																				●		
animals										●			●			●						
bathing	●																					
bedtime														●								
clothing						●				●					●							
clouds												●										
colors		●			●					●	●		●			●			●			
counting					●																	●
days of the week				●																		
dwellings									●													
farm																		●				
food		●		●				●			●									●		
friendship			●																			
growing up			●														●					
mice								●			●											
pairs																			●			
poetry															●				●			
rebus						●															●	
rhyme							●							●					●			
seasons						●									●							
spiders							●															
travel																					●	

Meeting Individual Needs

Often, even the best lessons do not meet the needs of *every* student in the class. The more proficient students finish quickly and get off task, while the less proficient students struggle and do not complete the task. Modify the lessons in this book to meet the needs of every student. Teach the same lesson but offer options such as the ones listed below.

ENGLISH LANGUAGE LEARNERS AND STRUGGLING LEARNERS

Support these students through the process of writing text innovations by

- meeting with them individually or in a small group to reread the class brainstorm list or chart

- asking them to dictate their chosen responses

- assisting them as they write their responses on their reproducible page

- listening to them read aloud their completed frame or reading it aloud with them

- encouraging them to echo as you read each page

GIFTED STUDENTS AND ADVANCED LEARNERS

Challenge these students by

- encouraging them to create and use creative ideas that are not listed on the class brainstorm list or chart

- demonstrating the use of descriptive words and expanded phrases to make their sentence(s) more interesting

- inviting them to read aloud their sentence(s) to a partner and listen as a partner reads aloud to them

- providing them with materials to create their own version of the book

100th Day Worries

Margery Cuyler
SIMON & SCHUSTER

While the other first graders are busy accumulating their collections of 100 things to celebrate the 100th day of school, Jessica is busy worrying. She does not have a hundred of anything. She comes up with a lot of ideas, but then rejects them all. A note from her mom in Jessica's lunchbox gives her a great idea—and provides the perfect way for the child to complete her assignment.

KEY WRITING SKILL: use specific details to focus on a topic

Prewriting

Write a large *100* on chart paper. Have the class discuss the things that the children in the book brought to school (e.g., peanuts, paper clips). Have students brainstorm a list of objects that could be brought to school, and write their responses on the 100 chart. Cut a piece of chart paper in the shape of a number 1. Invite students to identify things there are only one of in the classroom. Record their responses on the number one chart.

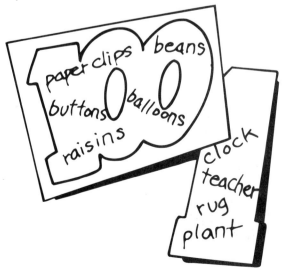

Writing

❶ Choose one of the items from the 100 chart (e.g., fish crackers).

❷ Verbally model your idea for completing the sentence frame. For example, say *On the 100th day of school, I'll bring 100 <u>fish crackers</u>.* Then, write your sentence on the chalkboard or chart paper.

❸ Choose a word from the number one chart to complete the second sentence (e.g., *There are hundreds of <u>fish crackers</u> but only one <u>clock</u>.*).

❹ Continue to model other sample sentences, as needed.

❺ Give each student a reproducible (page 12). Have students choose an item from each chart to complete their sentence frames.

❻ Invite students to illustrate their sentences.

❼ Make a copy of The 100th Day of School cover (page 13). Combine students' completed pages and the cover to make a class book.

On the 100th day of school, I'll bring 100

_____

_ _

_____ .

_____

_ _ _ _ _ _ _ _ _ _ _

There are hundreds of _____

_____

_ _ _ _ _ _ _ _ _ _

but only one _____ .

By _____

Developing Young Authors • K–1 © 2001 Creative Teaching Press

The 100th

Day of School

Written and illustrated by _____

We read *100th Day Worries* by Margery Cuyler.

The Bag I'm Taking to Grandma's

Shirley Neitzel

GREENWILLOW BOOKS

Shirley Neitzel uses rebuses and repetitive phrases to describe how a young boy packs a bag to visit his grandmother. He fills his bag with toys and other items that he feels are necessary to bring along. The book vividly points out the difference between a parent's and a child's view of what is necessary.

KEY WRITING SKILL: use specific details to focus on a topic

Prewriting

Have the class discuss the things the boy put in the bag he was taking to Grandma's house (e.g., mitt, toy cars). Ask students to brainstorm a list of things they would want to bring to school and things they would need to bring to school. Draw on the chalkboard or chart paper a T-chart with the headings *Need* and *Want*. Record each student response in the appropriate column. Discuss the difference between needs and wants.

Need	Want
pencil	toy
book	jump rope
paper	game
lunch	

Writing

1. Choose an object from the *Need* column of the chart (e.g., pencil).

2. Verbally model your idea for completing the sentence frame. For example, say *Here is my pencil that I'll pack in the bag I'm taking to school.* Then, write your sentence on the chalkboard or chart paper.

3. Continue to model other sample sentences, as needed.

4. Give each student a reproducible (page 15). Have students choose an object from the chart to complete their sentence frame.

5. Invite students to draw a picture of their item.

6. Make a copy of The Bag I'm Taking to School cover (page 16). Combine students' completed pages and the cover to make a class book.

Here is the bag I'm taking to school.

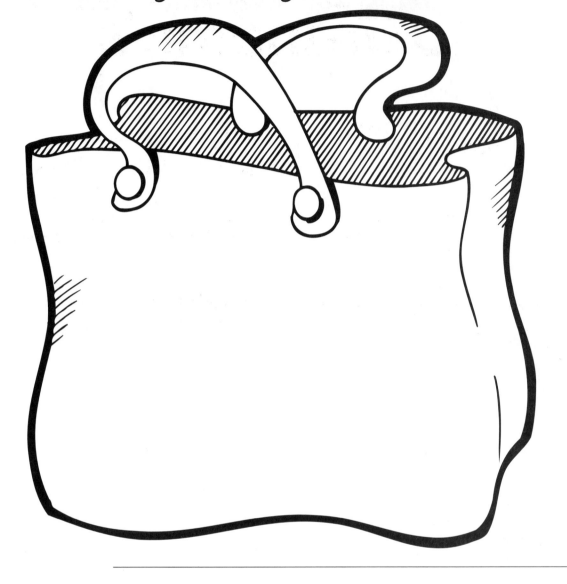

_____

Here is my _____

that I'll pack in the  I'm taking to school.

By _____

The Bag I'm Taking to School

Written and illustrated by

_____

We read *The Bag I'm Taking to Grandma's* by Shirley Neitzel.

Developing Young Authors • K–1 © 2001 Creative Teaching Press

Eating the Alphabet: Fruits & Vegetables from A to Z

Lois Ehlert

HARCOURT

Lois Ehlert introduces readers to a variety of fruits and vegetables from A (apricot, avocado, apple) to Z (zucchini). Each page of the book contains a clearly labeled watercolor collage of the various fruits and vegetables. This book also includes a glossary with information about each fruit and vegetable.

KEY WRITING SKILL: use specific details to focus on a topic

Prewriting

Discuss how Lois Ehlert's book names foods that begin with each letter of the alphabet. Tell students they are going to write an alphabet book on a new topic. Choose a topic (e.g., animals), and have students brainstorm things that relate to the topic that begin with each letter of the alphabet. Record their responses on the chalkboard or chart paper.

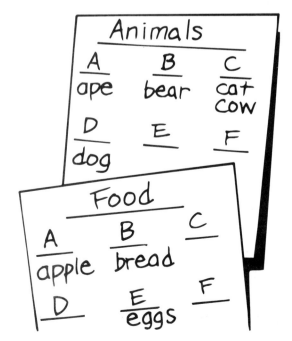

Writing

❶ Choose an animal from the brainstorm list (e.g., dog).

❷ Verbally model your idea for completing the sentence frame. For example, say _D is for dog_. Then, write your sentence on the chalkboard or chart paper.

❸ Continue to model other sample sentences, as needed.

❹ Give each student a reproducible (page 18). Assign each student a different letter of the alphabet. Have students complete the sentence frame for their assigned letter. If you have more than 26 students, have some students work with a partner. If you have less than 26 students, ask students who finish early to complete an additional page.

❺ Invite students to illustrate their sentence.

❻ Make a copy of the An Alphabet Book about ___ cover (page 19). Write the topic on the blank line to complete the cover title. Combine students' completed pages and the cover to make a class book.

_____ is for _____ .

By _____

Developing Young Authors • K–1 © 2001 Creative Teaching Press

An Alphabet Book about

Written and illustrated by

We read Eating the Alphabet: Fruits & Vegetables from A to Z by Lois Ehlert.

Developing Young Authors • K–1 © 2001 Creative Teaching Press

Some Things Go Together

Charlotte Zolotow

HarperCollins

What kinds of things go together? Charlotte Zolotow shows examples of things that go together: franks with beans, kings with queens, sand with sea, and me with you! Readers will enjoy hearing the rhythm of the words and identifying the connection between each pair of objects.

KEY WRITING SKILL: use specific details to focus on a topic

Prewriting

Discuss the things that go together in the book (e.g., hats with heads, pillows with beds). Give students a variety of magazines to look through. Encourage students to find pictures of things that go together. Ask each student to cut out two pictures of things that go together. Write on chart paper the title *Things That Go Together*. Invite the class to glue their pictures on the chart paper to create a visual brainstorm chart of things that go together. Use a black marker to label the pictures.

Writing

1. Choose one pair of items from the brainstorm chart (e.g., cookies with milk).

2. Verbally model your idea for completing the sentence frame. For example, say *Some things go together . . . cookies with milk*. Then, write your sentence on the chalkboard or chart paper.

3. Continue to model other sample sentences, as needed.

4. Give each student a reproducible (page 21). Have students choose a pair of items from the brainstorm chart to complete their sentence frame.

5. Invite students to draw a picture of their pair.

6. Make a copy of the Things That Go Together cover (page 22). Combine students' completed pages and the cover to make a class book.

Some things go together . . .

_____   _____

_____

_____ with _____

and ME with YOU!

By _____

Things That Go Together

Written and illustrated by

_____

We read *Some Things Go Together* by Charlotte Zolotow.

When Cows Come Home

David L. Harrison
BOYDS MILLS PRESS

When cows come home at the end of the day, they switch their tails and gently sway. At least, that's what they do when the farmer is looking. When he looks the other way, the cows play tag, swim in the pond, play the fiddle, ride bikes, square dance, and somersault in the fields.

KEY WRITING SKILLS: use specific details to focus on a topic, use descriptive words

Prewriting

Have the class discuss all the things the cows did in the story at the end of the day (e.g., gently sway, fiddle their fiddles). Create a brainstorm list of things that students do at the end of their day by inviting students to role-play. Choose one child to role-play an action (e.g., read a book), and encourage the rest of the class to guess what that student is doing. Record each correct answer on the chalkboard or chart paper. Invite other students to role-play different actions.

- read a book
- ride my bike
- call my grandma

Writing

❶ Choose an action from the brainstorm list (e.g., read a book).

❷ Verbally model your idea for completing the sentence frame. For example, say *When I come home at the end of the day, I read a book*. Then, write your sentence on the chalkboard or chart paper.

❸ Continue to model other sample sentences, as needed.

❹ Give each student a reproducible (page 24). Have students choose an action from the brainstorm list to complete their sentence frame.

❺ Invite students to illustrate their sentence.

❻ Make a copy of the Our "End of the Day" Stories cover (page 25). Combine students' completed pages and the cover to make a class book.

When I come home at the end of the day, I

_____

\- \-

_____

_____

\- \-

_____ .

By _____

Our "End of the Day" Stories

Written and illustrated by

_____

We read *When Cows Come Home* by David L. Harrison.

When I Get Bigger

Mercer Mayer

GOLDEN BOOKS PUBLISHING

Little Critter tells us all the things he will do when he is big enough to go to first grade. This includes everything from helping little kids on the swings to camping out in the backyard. By the end of his daydreaming, Little Critter is so tired he has to go to bed. As he himself admits, "I'm not bigger yet."

KEY WRITING SKILL: use specific details to focus on a topic

Prewriting

Have the class discuss the things that the character says he will do when he gets bigger (e.g., tell time, get a paper route). Invite an older group of students to visit your class to tell about some of the things that they like to do. Ask the older students what they do at home, at school, and with their friends. Record their responses on the chalkboard or chart paper. After they leave, have younger students add more ideas to the brainstorm list.

Writing

❶ Choose an idea from the brainstorm list (e.g., learn multiplication).

❷ Verbally model your idea for completing the sentence frames. For example, say *When I get bigger, I'll learn multiplication. I'll go to 2nd grade.* Then, write your sentences on the chalkboard or chart paper.

❸ Continue to model other sample sentences, as needed.

❹ Give each student a reproducible (page 27). Have students choose an idea from the brainstorm list to complete the first sentence frame. Ask students to write the grade they will be in the following year to complete the second sentence frame.

❺ Invite students to illustrate their sentences.

❻ Make a copy of the When I Get Bigger cover (page 28). Combine students' completed pages and the cover to make a class book.

When I get bigger, I'll _____

_____

_____

_____ .

I'll go to _____ grade.

By _____

When I Get Bigger

Written and illustrated by

_____

We read *When I Get Bigger* by Mercer Mayer.

Brown Bear, Brown Bear, What Do You See?

Bill Martin Jr.

HENRY HOLT AND COMPANY

This story has been a favorite of children for many years. Brown Bear sees Red Bird who sees Yellow Duck and so the story continues until a teacher asks a group of children what they see. The two-page spread at the end of the book features each color animal from the story.

KEY WRITING SKILLS: use adjectives, use repetitive sentence patterns

Prewriting

Have the class discuss what each animal saw (e.g., a purple cat, a white dog). Draw a pair of large eyes near the top of a piece of chart paper. Have students brainstorm who may be looking at them. Record their responses under the big eyes on the chart paper.

Writing

1. Choose a student name and a person from the brainstorm list (e.g., the principal).

2. Verbally model your idea for completing the sentence frames. For example, say *Sarah, Sarah, What do you see? I see the principal looking at me.* Then, write your sentences on the chalkboard or chart paper.

3. Continue to model other sample sentences, as needed.

4. Give each student a reproducible (page 30). Have students write their name on the first two blank lines. Then, ask them to choose a person from the brainstorm list to complete their second sentence frame.

5. Invite students to illustrate their sentences.

6. Complete the teacher reproducible (page 31) to use as the last page of the class book.

7. Make a copy of the Room __, Room__, What Do You See? cover (page 32). Write your room number on the blank lines to complete the title. Combine students' completed pages, your page, and the cover to make a class book.

_____

- -

_____,

name

_____

- -

_____,

name

What do you see?

_____

- -

I see _____

looking at me.

Teacher, Teacher, What do you see?

I see a wonderful class looking at me!

Room ___,
Room ___,
What Do You See?

Written and illustrated by

_____

We read *Brown Bear, Brown Bear, What Do You See?* by Bill Martin Jr.

Developing Young Authors • K–1 © 2001 Creative Teaching Press

Caps, Hats, Socks, and Mittens

Louise Borden

SCHOLASTIC

In an exuberant trip through the four seasons, readers discover many wonderful things about fall, winter, spring, and summer. The sensory descriptions will help readers understand the type of weather and things that happen in each season.

KEY WRITING SKILLS: use adjectives and/or descriptive details, explicitly state the theme

Prewriting

Discuss the words the author uses to describe each season. Have students look through other books about seasons to learn about things that are associated with each season. Title four separate pieces of chart paper *Winter, Spring, Summer,* and *Fall.* Ask students to generate a list of things associated with each season. Record each response on the appropriate paper.

Writing

1. Choose one item from the winter brainstorm list (e.g., snowflakes).

2. Verbally model your idea for completing the sentence frame. For example, say *Winter is snowflakes.* Then, write your sentence on the chalkboard or chart paper.

3. Continue to model other sample sentences, as needed.

4. Give each student a winter reproducible (page 34). Have students choose an idea from the winter brainstorm list to complete their sentence frame.

5. Invite students to illustrate their sentence.

6. Make a copy of the Winter is . . . cover (page 36). Combine students' completed pages and the cover to make a class book.

7. Repeat the writing activity for each of the other three seasons.

Fall is leaves changing colors. Fall is

_____

‑ ‑ ‑ ‑ ‑ ‑ ‑ ‑ ‑ ‑ ‑ ‑ ‑ ‑ ‑ ‑ ‑ ‑

_____ .

By _____

✂‑ ‑

Winter is caps, hats, socks, and mittens.

_____

‑ ‑ ‑ ‑ ‑ ‑ ‑ ‑ ‑ ‑ ‑ ‑ ‑ ‑ ‑ ‑ ‑ ‑

Winter is _____ .

By _____

Developing Young Authors • K–1 © 2001 Creative Teaching Press

Spring is plants in pots. Spring is

_____

- - - - - - - - - - - - - - - - - - - -

_____ .

By _____

- ✂

Summer is hot, hot, hot. Summer is

_____

- - - - - - - - - - - - - - - - - - - -

_____ .

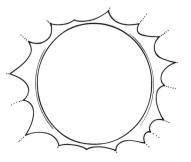

By _____

We read *Caps, Hats, Socks, and Mittens*
by Louise Borden.

Written and illustrated by _____

✂ -

We read *Caps, Hats, Socks, and Mittens*
by Louise Borden.

Written and illustrated by _____

Developing Young Authors • K–1 © 2001 Creative Teaching Press

We read *Caps, Hats, Socks, and Mittens*
by Louise Borden.

Written and illustrated by _____

--- ✂

We read *Caps, Hats, Socks, and Mittens*
by Louise Borden.

Written and illustrated by _____

Goodnight Moon

Margaret Wise Brown

HarperCollins

A little bunny is tucked away in a bed. One by one, the little bunny says good-night to all the familiar things in the room. Readers will enjoy hearing the rhythmic text and can have additional fun by searching for the little mouse on each page of the book.

KEY WRITING SKILLS: use descriptive details, use specific details to focus on a topic

Prewriting

Cut a piece of chart paper in the shape of a sun to create a word bank. Have students recall all the things to which the little bunny said goodnight (e.g., toy house, two little kittens). Invite students to brainstorm things that they might say good morning to when they come into the classroom. Use words and pictures to record their responses on the "sun."

Writing

1. Choose two objects from the word bank (e.g., clock and flag).

2. Verbally model your idea for completing the sentence frames. For example, say *Good morning classroom. Good morning <u>clock</u> and good morning <u>flag</u>.* Then, write your sentences on the chalkboard or chart paper.

3. Continue to model other sample sentences, as needed.

4. Give each student a reproducible (page 39). Have students choose two objects from the brainstorm list to complete their sentence frame.

5. Invite students to illustrate their sentence.

6. Make a copy of the Good Morning Classroom! cover (page 40). Combine students' completed pages and the cover to make a class book.

Good morning classroom.

_____

- - - - - - - - - - - - - - - - -

Good morning _____

and

_____

- - - - - - - - - - - - - - - - -

good morning _____.

By _____

Good Morning Classroom!

Written and illustrated by

_____

We read *Goodnight Moon* by Margaret Wise Brown.

I Went Walking

Sue Williams

HARCOURT

A walk around the farmyard becomes an exuberant event for the small child featured in this repetitive tale. During the course of the walk, the child identifies animals of different colors, including a brown horse, a red cow, a green duck, and a pink pig. Each animal joins the child and the walk ends in a joyous romp.

KEY WRITING SKILL: use descriptive details

Prewriting

Have the class discuss the different things that the boy saw on his walk (e.g., green duck, yellow dog). Take the class on a walk around the school or classroom. Invite students to talk about all the things that they see on the walk. Return to the classroom, and draw on the chalkboard or chart paper a T-chart with the headings *Object* and *Descriptive Word*. Have students brainstorm a list of the things they saw on the walk. Also, ask them to list a word that describes each object. Record their responses on the T-chart.

Object	Descriptive Word
tree	tall
penny	shiny
sky	blue

Writing

❶ Choose an object and its describing word from the T-chart (e.g., tree, tall).

❷ Verbally model your idea for completing the sentence frame. For example, say *I saw a tree as tall as can be!* Then, write your sentence on the chalkboard or chart paper.

❸ Continue to model other sample sentences, as needed.

❹ Give each student a reproducible (page 42). Have students use a pair of words from the T-chart to complete their sentence frame.

❺ Invite students to draw a picture of their object.

❻ Make a copy of the I Went Walking cover (page 43). Combine students' completed pages and the cover to make a class book.

I went walking . . .

What did I see? I saw

as

as can be!

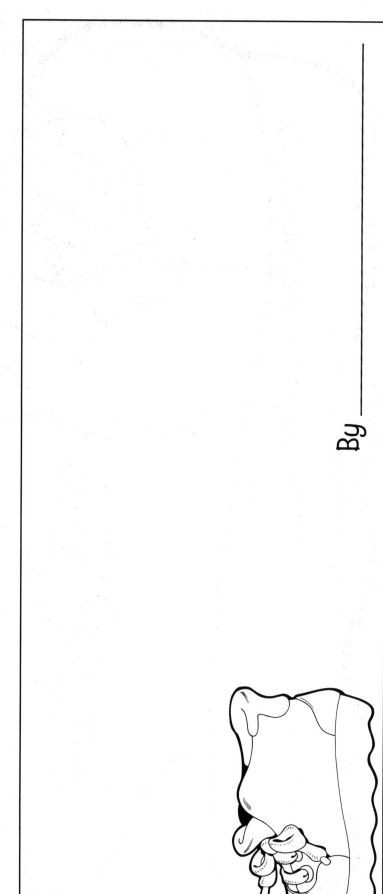

By

Developing Young Authors • K–1 © 2001 Creative Teaching Press

Written and illustrated by

We read *I Went Walking* by Sue Williams.

I Went Walking

It Looked Like Spilt Milk

Charles G. Shaw

HARPERTROPHY

Charles G. Shaw stimulates the imagination by leaving the reader guessing as to what all those white shapes could possibly be. Sometimes it looked like a birthday cake or an ice cream cone. But it wasn't either of them, so what could it be?

KEY WRITING SKILLS: use descriptive details, use interesting words, use pictures to help convey meaning

Prewriting

Have the class discuss the shapes presented in the story (e.g., a mitten, an angel). Cut a piece of chart paper in the shape of a cloud. Encourage students to brainstorm other things that clouds can look like. Record their responses on the "cloud."

snowman
ice-cream cone
mitten

Writing

1. Choose an item from the brainstorm list (e.g., flower).

2. Verbally model your idea for completing the sentence frames. For example, say *Sometimes it looked like* <u>a flower</u>. *But it wasn't* <u>a flower</u>. *It was just a cloud in the sky.* Then, write your sentences on the chalkboard or chart paper.

3. Continue to model other sample sentences, as needed.

4. Give each student a reproducible (page 45). Have students choose an item from the brainstorm list to complete their sentence frames. Ask students to use a blue crayon to color the cloud shape. (This will indicate the sky.) Give each student a 3" x 5" (7.5 cm x 12.5 cm) piece of white paper. Invite students to tear their paper to form their "cloud" and glue the cloud on to the "sky." (Or, have students make their cloud out of cotton balls.)

5. Make a copy of the Our Cloud Stories cover (page 46). Combine students' completed pages and the cover to make a class book.

I saw a cloud up in the sky. Sometimes it looked

_____

like _____ .

But it wasn't _____ .

It was just a cloud in the sky.

By _____

Our Cloud Stories

Written and illustrated by

_____

We read *It Looked Like Spilt Milk* by Charles G. Shaw.

Developing Young Authors • K–1 © 2001 Creative Teaching Press

Lunch

Denise Fleming

HENRY HOLT AND COMPANY

A hungry mouse peeks out of its hole and discovers a table of colorful fruits and vegetables. Readers will anticipate which fruit or vegetable comes next as the rodent munches his way through yellow corn, green peas, orange carrots, and the rest of the colorful foods

KEY WRITING SKILL: use adjectives and/or descriptive details

Prewriting

Have the class discuss the things that the mouse ate (e.g., tasty orange carrots). Draw on the chalkboard or chart paper a three-column chart with the headings *Describing Word, Color,* and *Food.* Have students brainstorm foods they like to eat. Ask them to list a describing word for and the color of each food. Record their responses in the appropriate columns of the chart.

Describing Word	Color	Food
crunchy	red	apple
crisp	green	pickle
sweet	pink	candy

Writing

❶ Choose a student name and one set of words from the brainstorm chart (e.g., crunchy, red, apple).

❷ Verbally model your idea for completing the sentence frames. For example, say *Matthew was very hungry. He ate a crunchy, red apple.* Then, write your sentences on the chalkboard or chart paper.

❸ Continue to model other sample sentences, as needed.

❹ Give each student a reproducible (page 48). Have students write their name to complete the first sentence. Ask them to use a set of words from the brainstorm chart to complete the second sentence frame.

❺ Invite students to illustrate their sentences.

❻ Make a copy of the Our Lunch Stories cover (page 49). Combine students' completed pages and the cover to make a class book.

_____

- -

_____ was very hungry.
name

_____   _____

- -

_____ ate _____ ,
He/She

_____   _____

- -

_____   _____ .

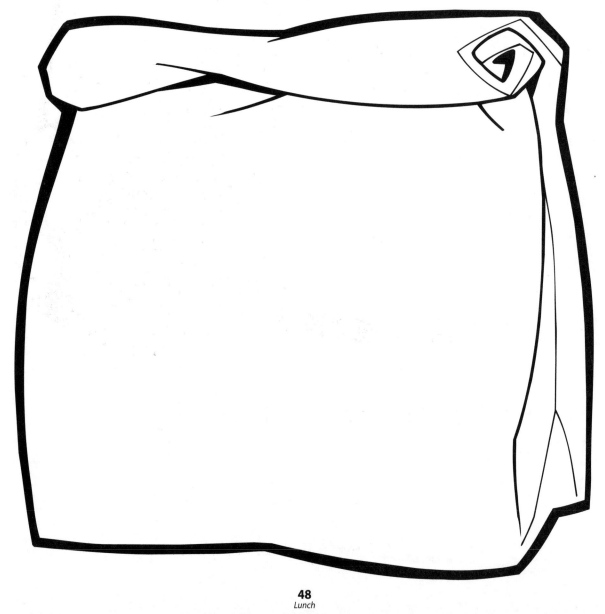

OUR LUNCH STORIES

Written and illustrated by

_____

We read *Lunch* by Denise Fleming.

Mary Wore Her Red Dress and Henry Wore His Green Sneakers

Merle Peek

CLARION BOOKS

On Katy's birthday, all of her animal friends come to her party dressed in clothes of different colors, from Mary in her red dress to Henry in his green sneakers. This book is a fun way for readers to learn about colors and animals.

KEY WRITING SKILL: use adjectives

Prewriting

Discuss what the characters in the story wore (e.g., Katy wore her yellow sweater). Have students brainstorm articles of clothing, and record their responses on the chalkboard or chart paper. Write the heading *Article of Clothing* at the top of that list. Then, ask them to name different colors. Record their responses under the heading *Color*.

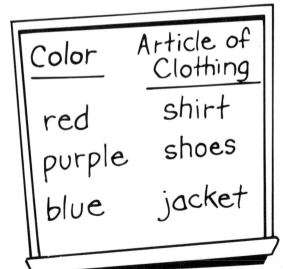

Color	Article of Clothing
red	shirt
purple	shoes
blue	jacket

Writing

❶ Choose a student name and a color and an article of clothing from the brainstorm lists (e.g., lavender blouse).

❷ Verbally model your idea for completing the sentence frame. For example, say *Rosa wore her lavender blouse all day long.* Then, write your sentence on the chalkboard or chart paper.

❸ Continue to model other sample sentences, as needed.

❹ Give each student a reproducible (page 51). Have students write their name on the first blank line. Then, ask them to choose a color and an article of clothing from the brainstorm lists to complete their sentence frame.

❺ Invite students to draw a picture of themselves in the clothing.

❻ Make a copy of the What Did We Wear? cover (page 52). Combine students' completed pages and the cover to make a class book.

name _____ wore _____ his/her _____

all day long.

What Did We Wear?

Written and illustrated by

_____

We read Mary Wore Her Red Dress and Henry Wore His Green Sneakers by Merle Peek.

A House Is a House for Me

Mary Ann Hoberman

VIKING

Mary Ann Hoberman's clever rhyming text covers every imaginable type of house for various people, animals, and objects.

From a husk is a house for a corn ear to a garage is a house for a car, readers will begin to think of all kinds of items that can be homes for someone or something.

KEY WRITING SKILLS: arrange ideas in a logical order, use repetitive sentence patterns

Prewriting

Have the class discuss the types of houses depicted in the book (e.g., hive, hole, web). Encourage students to name who lives in each type of home (e.g., an ant lives in a hole). Give each student two 3" (7.5 cm) squares of white paper. Have students draw a picture of an animal on one square and the animal's home on the other square. Label each picture, and then display the pictures on a bulletin board to create a thematic word wall that students can use for other writing projects. Title the display *A House Is a House for Whom?*

Writing

1. Choose a house and its inhabitant from the word wall (e.g., hive and bee).

2. Verbally model your idea for completing the sentence frame. For example, say *A hive is a house for a bee. A house is a house for me!* Then, write your sentences on the chalkboard or chart paper.

3. Continue to model other sample sentences, as needed.

4. Give each student a reproducible (page 54). Have students choose a house and its inhabitant from the word wall to complete their sentence frame.

5. Invite students to illustrate their sentence.

6. Make a copy of the A House Is a House for Whom? cover (page 55). Combine students' completed pages and the cover to make a class book.

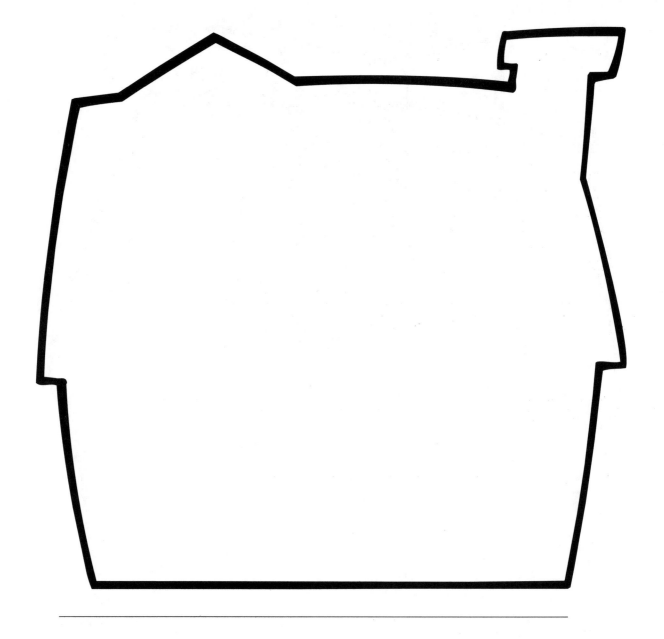

A _____ is a

_____

house for a _____.

A house is a house for me!

By _____

Developing Young Authors • K–1 © 2001 Creative Teaching Press

A House Is a House for Whom?

Written and illustrated by

_____

We read *A House Is a House for Me* by Mary Ann Hoberman.

If You Give a Mouse a Cookie

Laura Joffe Numeroff

HarperCollins

What will happen if you give a mouse a cookie? He'll ask for a glass of milk, and then he'll need a straw, a napkin, and so on. Each item prompts the need for another. Readers will be entertained by this story of how one simple event can trigger other thoughts and events.

KEY WRITING SKILLS: arrange ideas in a logical order, write about personal experiences

Prewriting

Discuss what happened when the mouse was given a cookie. Create a three-column grid on the chalkboard or chart paper. Label the columns *Animal, Thing,* and *Need or Want.* Have a student volunteer name an animal (e.g., lion). Then, ask another student to name something that he or she would give that animal (e.g., pizza). Ask the class what the lion would need or want after it had the pizza (e.g., soda). Write their responses in the appropriate columns of the grid. Invite students to brainstorm more ideas to fill the grid.

Animal	Thing	Need or Want
lion	pizza	soda
cat	piece of paper	crayons
fox	blanket	pillow

Writing

1. Choose a row of words from the grid (e.g., lion, pizza, soda).

2. Verbally model your idea for completing the sentence frame. For example, say *If you give a lion a pizza, she will ask for a soda.* Then, write your sentence on the chalkboard or chart paper.

3. Continue to model other sample sentences, as needed.

4. Give each student a reproducible (page 57). Have students choose a row of words from the grid to complete their sentence frame.

5. Invite students to illustrate their sentence.

6. Make a copy of the If You Give an Animal Something cover (page 58). Combine students' completed pages and the cover to make a class book.

If you give a _____

_____ _____

a _____ , _____
he/she

_____

will ask for _____ .

By _____

If You Give an Animal Something

Written and illustrated by

_____

We read *If You Give a Mouse a Cookie* by Laura Joffe Numeroff.

The Itsy Bitsy Spider

Retold by Iza Trapani

WHISPERING COYOTE PRESS

In a fresh retelling, Iza Trapani lets us follow the itsy bitsy spider through a series of adventures. After the traditional verse of going up the waterspout, the spider continues its adventure by climbing up a kitchen wall, a pail, and a rocking chair. The spider's final destination is a tree where it spins a web.

KEY WRITING SKILLS: arrange ideas in a logical order, use pictures to help convey meaning

Prewriting

Draw a large spiderweb on chart paper and a large ladder on another piece of chart paper. Have students recall the different things that the itsy bitsy spider climbed (e.g., waterspout, chair). Write their responses on the web. Invite students to brainstorm other objects the little spider could attempt to climb, and record those responses too. Next, have students brainstorm objects that they themselves can climb, and record their responses on the ladder.

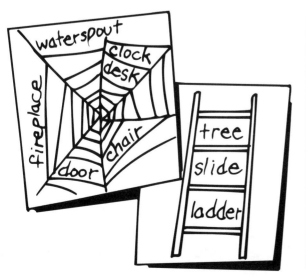

Writing

❶ Choose an object from each chart (e.g., clock and tree).

❷ Verbally model your idea for completing the sentence frames. For example, say *The itsy bitsy spider climbed up a clock. I can climb up a tree.* Then, write your sentences on the chalkboard or chart paper.

❸ Continue to model other sample sentences, as needed.

❹ Give each student a reproducible (page 60). Have students choose an object from each chart to complete their sentence frames.

❺ Invite students to illustrate their sentences.

❻ Make a copy of The Itsy Bitsy Spider and Me cover (page 61). Combine students' completed pages and the cover to make a class book.

The itsy bitsy spider climbed up _____

_____

_____.

_____

I can climb up _____

_____

_____.

By _____

The Itsy Bitsy Spider and Me

Written and illustrated by

_____

We read *The Itsy Bitsy Spider* retold by Iza Trapani.

The Jacket I Wear in the Snow

Shirley Neitzel

GREENWILLOW BOOKS

In this story, Shirley Neitzel uses a repetitive pattern to describe getting ready to go out in the snow. A little *girl* introduces each piece of winter clothing that she puts on before going out in the snow. By the time she is dressed and ready, she has on such a bundle of layers that she can hardly move.

KEY WRITING SKILLS: arrange ideas chronologically, use sequence words

Prewriting

Discuss the various articles of clothing mentioned in the book. Have students brainstorm the kinds of clothes they wear to school. Record student responses on the chalkboard or chart paper under the heading *Article of Clothing*. Then, have students brainstorm a list of colors, and write those words under the heading *Color*.

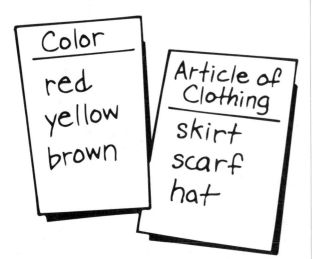

Color
red
yellow
brown

Article of Clothing
skirt
scarf
hat

Writing

❶ Choose a color and an article of clothing from the brainstorm lists (e.g., green scarf).

❷ Verbally model your idea for completing the sentence frame. For example, say *This is the green scarf I wear to school.* Then, write your sentence on the chalkboard or chart paper.

❸ Continue to model other sample sentences, as needed.

❹ Give each student a reproducible (page 63). Have students choose a color and an article of clothing from the brainstorm lists to complete their sentence frame.

❺ Invite students to illustrate their sentence.

❻ Make a copy of The Clothes I Wear to School cover (page 64). Combine students' completed pages and the cover to make a class book.

This is the _____

_____ I wear to school.

By _____

The Clothes I Wear to School

Written and illustrated by

_____

We read *The Jacket I Wear in the Snow* by Shirley Neitzel.

Ten Black Dots

Donald Crews
MULBERRY BOOKS

What can you do with ten black dots? Just about anything! In this unique counting book, Donald Crews shows how one dot can make a sun, two dots can make the eyes of a fox, and three dots can make a snowman's face. And that's just the beginning!

KEY WRITING SKILLS: arrange ideas in a logical order, use pictures to help convey meaning, focus on the main idea by narrowing a general topic to a more specific one

Prewriting

Have the class discuss the things that were made from the black dots in the book (e.g., three dots made a snowman's face). Create a ten-column grid on the chalkboard or chart paper. Label the columns from *One Dot* to *Ten Dots*. Have students brainstorm objects they could create using dots. Record each response in the appropriate column. Draw pictures of their responses to provide students with visual clues.

Writing

❶ Choose an object from the first column of the brainstorm list (e.g., an eye).

❷ Verbally model your idea for completing the sentence frame. For example, say *One black dot can make an eye*. Then, write your sentence on the chalkboard or chart paper.

❸ Continue to model other sample sentences, as needed.

❹ Make one copy of the "one" reproducible (page 66) and nine copies of the "two–ten" reproducible (page 67) for each student. Make a copy of the Ten Black Dots cover (page 68) for each student. Staple together each set of pages to make a booklet.

❺ Give each student a booklet and a page of adhesive black dots. Encourage students to put the appropriate number of black dots on each page.

❻ Invite students to complete each sentence frame and illustrate their sentences.

❼ OPTION: Assign each student a number from one to ten. Give one reproducible page to each student to complete. Use the completed pages to make two or three class books.

One black dot can make _____ .

Developing Young Authors • K–1 © 2001 Creative Teaching Press

black dots can make

Ten Black Dots

Written and illustrated by _____

We read _Ten Black Dots_ by Donald Crews.

Developing Young Authors • _K–1_ © 2001 Creative Teaching Press

The Very Hungry Caterpillar

Eric Carle
PHILOMEL

One Sunday, a very hungry caterpillar hatched. Throughout the week, it eats its way through a variety of colorful foods before getting a stomachache. Then, the caterpillar eats a leaf, spins a cocoon, and emerges as a beautiful butterfly.

KEY WRITING SKILLS: arrange ideas in a logical order, create a simple beginning and ending

Prewriting

Recall all the foods eaten by the very hungry caterpillar (e.g., apple, pickle, Swiss cheese). Have students brainstorm other foods that they ate last week. Give each student a 3" (7.5 cm) square of paper. Invite students to draw a picture of a food that they ate. Divide a large piece of chart paper into five columns. Label each column with one of the following: *Breads and Cereal, Meats, Fruits and Vegetables, Dairy*, and *Fats and Sweets*. Use a black marker to label the food on each child's square. Ask each student to tape his or her square in the appropriate column of the food chart.

Writing

❶ Choose a student name and two items from the food chart (e.g., chicken and ice cream).

❷ Verbally model your idea for completing the sentence frames. For example, say *Last week, Maria, the very hungry student, ate chicken and ice cream. After that, Maria felt much better!* Then, write your sentences on the chalkboard or chart paper.

❸ Give each student a reproducible (page 70). Have students write their name in the appropriate spaces. Then, ask them to choose two items from the food chart to complete their sentence frame.

❹ Invite students to draw their two food items.

❺ Make a copy of The Very Hungry Student cover (page 71). Combine students' completed pages and the cover to make a class book.

Last week, _____, the very
name

hungry student, ate _____

_____

and _____.

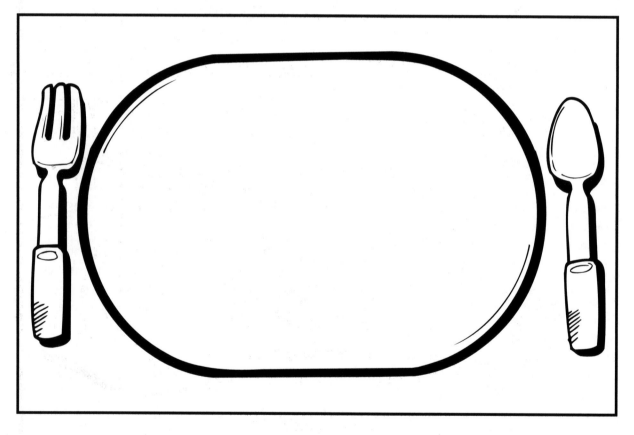

After that, _____ felt
name

much better!

Developing Young Authors • K–1 © 2001 Creative Teaching Press

THE VERY HUNGRY STUDENT

Written and illustrated by

_____

We read *The Very Hungry Caterpillar* by Eric Carle.

When I Was Five

Arthur Howard

HARCOURT

A boy describes his aspirations, his favorite things, and his best friend, back when he was five. But now that he is *six*, all his preferences have changed slightly.

Now he likes race cars and wants to be a famous baseball player or a deep-sea diver. One thing that has not changed though is his best friend.

KEY WRITING SKILLS: arrange ideas chronologically, write about personal experiences

Prewriting

Discuss what the boy in the book wanted to be when he was five. Then, discuss the things that he wanted to be when he turned six (e.g., a baseball player or a deep-sea diver). Have students brainstorm occupations that they are interested in being now that they are growing up. Record their responses on the chalkboard or chart paper.

Writing

1. Choose two occupations from the brainstorm list (e.g., baseball player and pilot).

2. Verbally model your idea for completing the sentence frames. For example, say *When I was four, I wanted to be a baseball player. Now I'm five, and I want to be a pilot.* Then, write your sentences on the chalkboard or chart paper.

3. Continue to model other sample sentences, as needed.

4. Give each student a reproducible (page 73). Have students choose two occupations from the brainstorm list to complete their sentence frames.

5. Invite students to illustrate their sentences.

6. Make a copy of the When I Was . . . cover (page 74). Combine students' completed pages and the cover to make a class book.

When I was _____,

I wanted to be _____.

Now I'm _____,

and I want to be _____.

By _____

Written and illustrated by

_____

We read *When I Was Five* by Arthur Howard.

Developing Young Authors • K–1 © 2001 Creative Teaching Press

Green Eggs and Ham

Dr. Seuss

RANDOM HOUSE

Sam-I-am is trying to get somebody to taste green eggs and ham. No matter how Sam-I-am presents the meal, everyone refuses. But Sam-I-am's persistence pays off when someone finally tastes the green eggs and ham and decides that it does taste delicious.

KEY WRITING SKILLS: use dialogue to show characters' thoughts and feelings, develop a strong character

Prewriting

Discuss colors and foods with the class. Talk about how color influences their food preferences. For example, ask *Would you eat a piece of blue bread?* Have students brainstorm a list of colors and a list of foods. Record their responses on the chalkboard or chart paper. Encourage students to combine a word from each list to create new "foods" (e.g., blue chicken).

blue
black
orange
magenta

carrots
chicken
tomatoes

Writing

1. Combine a color and a food from the brainstorm lists (e.g., blue carrots).

2. Verbally model your idea for completing the sentence frames. For example, say *I am Ms. Jones. I do not like blue carrots.* Then, write your sentences on the chalkboard or chart paper.

3. Continue to model other sample sentences, as needed.

4. Give each student a reproducible (page 76). Have students write their name on the first blank line and choose a color and a food item from the brainstorm lists to complete the second sentence frame.

5. Glue a photo of each student on his or her reproducible page.

6. Invite students to draw their food.

7. Make a copy of the We Will Not Eat Them Anywhere! cover (page 77). Combine students' completed pages and the cover to make a class book.

_____

- -

I am _____.

name

Glue student's
photo here.

_____

- -

I do not like _____.

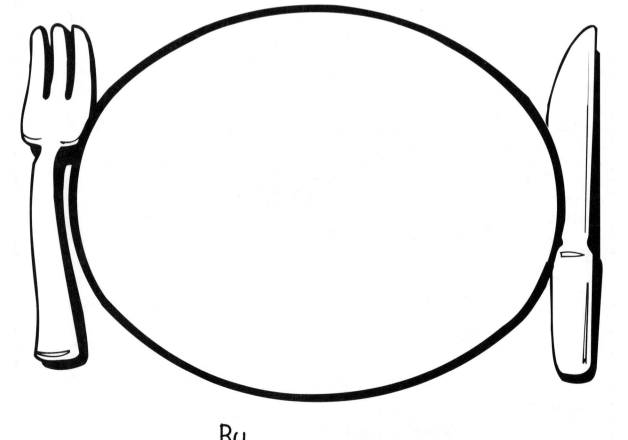

By _____

We Will Not Eat Them Anywhere!

Written and illustrated by

_____

We read *Green Eggs and Ham* by Dr. Seuss.

King Bidgood's in the Bathtub

Audrey Wood

HARCOURT

This playful tale is about a fun-loving king who refuses to leave his bathtub and attend to his duties. One by one, the knight, the queen, the duke, and all the members of the court attempt to persuade the king to leave his bath. Rather than leave the tub to perform his duties, the king completes each task in the bathtub. Finally, the clever page comes up with an idea that gets the king out of the bathtub.

KEY WRITING SKILL: use dialogue to show characters' thoughts and feelings

Prewriting

Discuss the different things that King Bidgood wanted to do in the bathtub (e.g., fish, eat lunch). Place a rug in the center of the floor. Tell students to pretend the rug is a bathtub. Invite students to take turns standing on the rug and pantomiming a creative thing they would do in the bathtub. Have the other students try to identify the action. Record the correct responses on the chalkboard or chart paper.

read a book
eat breakfast
dance

Writing

❶ Choose a student name and an activity from the brainstorm list (e.g., eat dessert).

❷ Verbally model your idea for completing the sentence frames. For example, say *"Help! Help! Kathy is in the bathtub and she won't get out! Oh, who knows what to do?" "Come in!" cried Kathy. "Today, we eat dessert in the tub!"* Then, write the sentences on the chalkboard or chart paper.

❸ Continue to model other sample sentences, as needed.

❹ Give each student a reproducible (page 79). Have students write their name to complete the first two sentences. Then, ask them to choose an activity from the brainstorm list to complete the last sentence frame.

❺ Invite students to illustrate their sentences.

❻ Make a copy of the Our Bathtub Book cover (page 80). Combine students' completed pages and the cover to make a class book.

"Help! Help! _____ is in

name

the bathtub and _____ won't get out!

he/she

Oh, who knows what to do?"

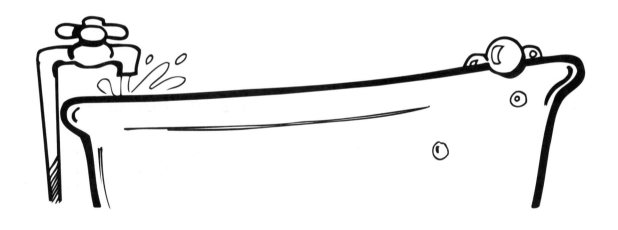

"Come in!" cried _____.

name

"Today, we _____
in the tub!"

Developing Young Authors • K–1 © 2001 Creative Teaching Press

Our Bathtub Book

Written and illustrated by

_____

We read *King Bidgood's in the Bathtub* by Audrey Wood.